# The Incredible Life of a French Gypsy

Provided to: Dawn Densmore-Parent

*Dedication*

# "To Brenda!"

*Many Thanks!*

*"Frenchy"*

Cover Design by: Tamara Smith, UVM Print and Mail, VT

©Copyright 2022

ISBN: 978-1-7342353-5-7

**INTRODUCTION**

This book is the result of a request from Claude D. "Frenchy" Mongeau to document his life's adventures.

His memories will astound and amaze you!

His journey begins with meeting one of the loves of his life, Brenda. He and she would eventually marry different people, but both would get to reconnect during the latter years of their lives!

Laugh and cry with him! His remarkable experiences brought him around the world to many different countries!

Dawn Densmore-Parent

# Contents

**MY BEGINNING** — 7
Chapter 1 – The Beginning — 7
Chapter 2 – My Gypsy Life — 19
Chapter 3 – Childhood Years — 21

**THE ARMY** — 23
Chapter 4 – Joining the Army — 23

**RE-ENLISTMENT** — 29
Chapter 5 – Re-Enlistment — 29

**OUR MOTTO** — 41
Chapter 6 – Above the Rest — 41

**ADVENTURES** — 43
Chapter 7 – Other Adventures — 43

**MY TRAVELS** — 45
Chapter 8 – New Mexico — 45

**THE DREAM COME TRUE** — 49
Chapter 9 – Hawaii — 49

**WAY UP NORTH!** — 53
Chapter 10 – Alaska — 53

**MY NEW CHAPTER** — 57
Chapter 11 – Beginning Again — 57

**BECOMING A BAKER** — 59
Chapter 12 – My New Life — 59

**STORM CLOUDS** — 61
Chapter 13 – My Biggest Trial — 61

**GOING HOME!** — 65
Chapter 14 - Full Circle — 65

Chapter 15 – LIFE LESSONS 67

# MY BEGINNING

## Chapter 1 – The Beginning

**My Dad and Mom**

This book contains the memories of many things that occurred throughout my life. I was born as a twin with my sister on January 8, 1945 in Saint Hyacinthe, P.O. Quebec, Canada. My family lived in St. Christine and we visited my grandma and grandpa's home often.

**My grandpa's home in St. Christine**

At three years old I remember 'nosing around' and 'sneaking' into the kitchen where Madame Vandall made potato slices on a stove burner. She would then put salt on them and give me little pieces to eat. My love for 'food' began early in life!

**I was born in St. Christine Quebec Canada**

I loved to 'run' down our hallway and then back to my bedroom through a room divider that was made from wood ropes with round balls of wood that hung in the doorway. At four years old I would help with little things like picking up wood for the stove.

**Our Sunday Dress Up**

I also would fetch water for Mrs. Vandall for her little green and white washing machine that had rollers that she would put the clothes through before hanging them outside to dry. My first haircut was done by Mr. Leblanch for .25 cents and my Dad took me to have that done.

Work Horses                    Our horses Queen and Dolly

I remember my Dad who we called 'the old man' say he was tired of working in the woods! He was paid $5 dollars a day there, and he knew they paid $8 dollars a day for work at the hospital! That was when we moved close to the LeBlanch store into an apartment that was located right across from the railroad station.

**WATCHING TRAINS!**

I loved to watch the trains come and go to Richmond. My Dad was beginning to 'buy' animals with my Uncle Ted, and they would be chasing women at the same time. All my life, the Mongeau men "Wilfred, Albert, Ted, Armand" loved life!

Before I was seven years old, we had moved a total of 4 times to 4 different farms. Saint Christine was my favorite because I can still recall the picture of the cattle truck which was a 1952 Fargo cattle truck. We used that truck when we left Saint Christine, Quebec on June 15, 1953. I was eight years old. We had two working horses named Queen and Dolly.

**The Cattle truck**

We moved to Vermont to a place called the BeeBee farm in Swanton, Vermont. This was a large Turkey farm where we plucked and plucked turkeys every day! But they had ponies too and I loved to ride them!

**The Beebe Farm**

The 'old man' got sick of that and he found a job in St. Albans in a place called the The Hill Farm.

**The Hill Farm**

The head boss of the Hill Farm was Mr. Lumbra and he lived in the 'Big House".

I was raised Catholic and each night at 7 pm we would get on our knees and listen to the Rosaire on the radio by Cardinal Paul Emil Legger from Montreal. How many kids do that today? My first communion with my sister was done when we were seven years old.

**My First Communion – me with my sister Claudette**

**Our confirmation pictures**

**Our green chevy car**

My Dad bought a 1953 Chevrolet that was green and a four-door sedan that was ugly. Green is the color that I now still hate. We used to go riding around in that car and park along the roads under the big maple trees. "You" had better go 'tinkle' before you left! My Dad would NEVER stop for you to go 'pee'.

Our first family picture was taken when I was 8 years old and my family used it on a Christmas card.

**Our first family Christmas Card**

One day my Dad showed up and said, "We're moving to Montgomery Center!" This was about thirty-five miles from St. Albans. He would go to work on a BIG dairy Farm owned by a 'well to do' farmer that he had met through his trips of buying and selling cows. It was called the Claude Marcy farm and had 600 acres of land and 125 cows that needed to be milked twice a day!

**Claude Marcy farm – Montgomery Center, VT & Me and My Dad Hauling Silage**

I still could not speak English. At that time, I was eight and a half. It would be the first time I would have to show up to go to School. Mrs. Lumbra, Mrs. Scott, Mrs. Rushford, and Mrs. Domina were the teachers.

I loved living in Montgomery Center to this day because it was the place that we stayed longer than any other place.

**Montgomery Farm**

We had a water dam on the farm, and I used to take a long stick with bailing twice and using old nuts and bolts as sinkers, I would go to the edge of the river where it was dammed up and catch BIG suckers. As a kid I didn't even like to 'fish' but I certainly loved catching these fish! There was a man who also fished there, Mr. Tatro. I would keep watch for him and every time there was a rainstorm, he would come to the same place as me to fish.

One day he said, "Next fish I get, I give to you!" Then all of a sudden, I saw his pole go down and he gently, with his fly rod, brought up a four-and-a-half pound Brook trout. It was as a beautiful fish! But I never did get that trout!

One day I decided to follow the stream down to the edge of town. There I saw a giant rock. I jumped 'rock to rock' and finally made it to the edge of that giant rock. I stuck my head out far enough where I could see 'monster suckers"! That became my favorite fishing spot and I hope someday to go there on my final run and drip my ashes to feed the suckers one last time!

## School

I spent the third grade through the seventh grade attending Holy Angels. I started the eighth grade there as well, but never got to finish. It was time to 'pack again' and move this time to Stoughton, Massachusetts. My Dad had gotten a new job on another BIG farm.

The Big shot who owned the farm, worked in Boston and his name was Charles McNamara. Farms there were little pieces of meadows here and there, not like we had in Vermont. I registered for school there and after a few weeks, 'the old man, said' "I only went to the 3$^{rd}$ grade! You're going to work on the farm!"

He got ma a job working with one of the sons of Charles McNamara. He told me, 'You're going to make $75 bucks a week!" Except when I got paid, I only could keep $5 of that! I can still see the little brown envelopes that contained the cash. Charles had two sons, and I worked my 'buns' off!

## The Girl

One day I saw this small blonde girl walking on the road. When I saw her, I went to see who she was. Her name was Christine. We chatted for a while. One of the workers said to me, "There you go, your first gal in Massachusetts!'

We used to go on Saturdays to the Chamberlain's House to sing and to dance. Christine brought her sister, Priscilla, and she was the love of my life! She was 3 years older than me, but I didn't care!

Priscilla was in Art School in Boston. When her parents found out that I was a farmer's son, they made her breakup with me.

Mr. Chamberlain drove a beautiful T-bird car that was all white. One day a French couple showed up to work with us from Newport, Vermont. The barn that I worked in was right across the barn yard.

Once a week, they would bring beer barley and drop it near their little house. The smell was so bad it reminded me of the 'Pea Vines" that we used to transport from Canada. When we got to the border, the juices from that truck were so bad that the border patrol officers would just 'wave' us through!

# BEING A GYPSY

## Chapter 2 – My Gypsy Life

These many different farms from Montgomery Center to East Berkshire, to East Enosburg, to West Enosburg, to Saint Albans to the farms in Massachusetts would cause us to be known as the 'French Gypsies".

My family could pick up and move quickly from place to place.
Our moves were made possible by North America Vanlines. Each time that we moved, the driver was always the same – Mr. LeBelle. We became friends until he passed away. During all my travels, I still go back and think about all the people that influenced my life.

Even with of all the moves, I am very proud to be able to show my Diploma in English and in French signed by Father Le Veer in 1960.

**Brenda**
I would meet my lifelong friend, Brenda, during the time I was enrolled at Holy Angels School. I went to school to see her. We were able to talk a little here and there when I was at school. She was on my mind, and in my thoughts. She had her wonderful smile and was easy for me to be

around. Unfortunately, my family's constant moving would prevent me from getting to really know her.

And my family's constant moving eventually disconnected us. When trying to reconnect with her, I would learn that she had left, and then, that she had married someone else. As life goes, I too would find and marry someone else. My visits back to Vermont would always include arranging to see Brenda, and we would meet for lunch. But again, she was married to someone else, and I was married to someone else! There was no way for me to know THEN how by God's Divine providence, we would be able to reconnect after so many decades during the latter years of our lives.

In 1961, when my family moved to 25 Allen Street in St. Albans, Vermont, the door opened for me to work at the Dairy Bar owned by an old friend of mind, Rege Boudreau.

Here, my entire life would take a major turn that would cause me to travel around the world. Two of my favorite clients were from the railroad, and I loved truckers who would stop in from all over for the great meals. Everything that we prepared was served for under $1 dollar.

# MY CHILDHOOD

## Chapter 3 – Childhood Years

**Me and my brother gathering sap for sugaring**

One of the farms in Massachusetts was located in South Durham, called the Willy Dunn Farm. Then we worked at the Saint Christine Martin farm. There we would chop rutabagas for the cows. This was very hard work because these are just like 'rocks' to cut, but I love them to this day!

Our family worked for several Vermont farmers:
In Montgomery,
East Berkshire,
West Enosburg,
and at the Enosburg Leach Farm.
We also did sugaring as kids which was a lot of hard work for us at a very young age.

We went to work 'commercial' but that lasted only two months.
Once back in St. Albans, we lived with Ed and Polly LaBrie on Allen Street by the railroad tracks.

One day I walked to the "Dairy Bar' and asked if anybody was looking for a person to work. They said, "We don't need your help!" The owner was in the basement and came up with lunch specials. He used to sell those lunch specials. I went to work the next day in the bake shop. I liked the place! We did not do fries, but we had great hash browns!

Once again, I was enrolled back at Holy Angels Convent in St. Albans to finish my eighth grade. Sister Emedy was the teacher.

I can still remember trying to sing, "Come along with me Lucille, in my merry Oldsmobile".

# THE ARMY

## Chapter 4 – Joining the Army

My job as night cook at the Dairy Center allowed me to work from 10 pm to 8 am. I loved it! The railroad men came in between 2 am and 4 am. Paul and his buddy liked my cooking. The truck drivers and I also became friends.

One night two of my new friends said to me, "Why don't you join the Service and make something of yourself!"

I saw an Army recruiter who came to my house and visited with my parents who had to sign the papers for my enlistment.

So, on March 2, 1962, I joined the Army. I left on a Greyhound bus going to Buffalo, New York. We would travel during the middle of the night and land in Columbia South Carolina, then onto Fort Jackson for the start of basic training. I was a 6 2 and then became a B 13 3.

**Me at Fort Jackson, Columbia, South Carolina**

There were eleven of us from Vermont and we all made it threw the basic training.

One day at the beer garden on Jack Ass Hill, we saw these 'cats' all shined up with 'berets and jump boots'. "Espri de genere' so we wanted to be like these 'cats'. We all signed up to go to Fort Benning, Georgia.
We used to go to the Soldiers Club. We would look like them! There was a song:

*"Bimbo Bimbo have you heard,*
*I'm going to jump from a big Iron Bird!*
*If the chute don't open, going to open my reserve,*
*if the reserve don't open, I'm going to lose my nerves   Whoa"*

We all made it into "Jump School". After graduation from Jump School, I went home on leave to Vermont. Then, I reported to my 101$^{st}$ Airborne

Division E Company 327th Infantry Brigade.

My first stop was to drop down and ask someone to give me $20. I was told, "You're not Airborne, and I was assigned to the fourth platoon as a radio operator and armor for Daddy Raider SFC Jungles.

We had a couple of 2nd lieutenants in our class. At graduation, on our way back to our barracks, one of the lieutenant's thought he was a leader now. He stopped us in front of the shack, where the instructors were located, and we yelled, "We want "Jap"! We want "Jap"!" Then "Jap" came out! He made all of us do 'push ups' until we could do no more and then sent us on our way!

**My First Wife Patsey**            **Our children Clarke & Cindy**

**Fort Gordon**

In Fort Gordon we made $55 more per month. At graduation, we were all sent to Fort Campbell, Kentucky or Fort Brag, North Carolina.

Across the river from Fort Campbell is Clarksville, Tennessee, and that is

where I met Patsey who would become my first wife. I met her at a roller rink in Clarksville, Tennessee. Her Mom worked as a seamstress across the street from us at Fort Campbell. We had two children, Clark and Cindy that were three years apart. When Clark was being born, I got tired of waiting around after ten hours and went to the A&W to get a burger and a soda. When I got back to the hospital at Fort Campbell, my mother-in-law hit me on the head with her purse and asked where'd you go?! My son Clarke was born while I was at the A&W.
We were going on different operations and one trip to Turkey.

I decided not to continue doing what I was doing. I told my Mess Sergeant Big John Mason, that I used to be a 'short order cook' back in Vermont.

Half of us were sent to the 327th Infantry by the Yomoto drop zone. I was with the half that was sent to E Company. Our moto was "Above the Rest!"

I was sent to the 4th platoon as a 'grant'. Outside the Barracks, I saw this big Black Sergeant. He came to us and said, "You're a 'peon' and you're wearing the big 'chockran jump boots." Then the 4th squad leader, Jerry Jungles came out and said, "You're going to be my radio man and armor." He was called "Daddy Raider". We went on many assignments. I hated to wear that ten radio everywhere. I felt like 'Jackie Gleason' saying "twenty-one fifty' to Headquarters.

Changes would come in what would seem like just 'overnight'. Daddy Raider would make it possible for me to be a cook and he made the arrangements. The Mess Sergeant Big John Mason was so bowlegged that you could drive a train through the middle of his legs.

We became the best of friends until he passed away twenty years later.

I loved the training in the Mohave Dessert and making biscuits on an M-59 Field range. We used a square pan with four dehydrated milk cans to elevate the pans so they would not burn.

**SP/5 Cook**

I became an SP/5 Cook and I loved it! There were new lieutenants that became Mess Officers. My new Mess Sergeant was Big John Mason. He could guzzle a gallon of beer from a mayonnaise jar and smack his lips. He was 'cool' and we all got along great!

On one of our trips, we were sent to Alabama where Martin Luther King was shot. That was where I became a good baker in a field range making biscuits for our SOS meals. Yummy, yummy, yummy – known as 'shit on a shingle'. There is nothing better than SOS with hot hash brown potatoes and hot sauce when you're freezing in the rain!

# RE-ENLISTMENT

## Chapter 5 – Re-Enlistment

In 1964, I signed up for four more years.

I got orders to be sent to Germany. My stay in Germany was cut short and I was sent back to the states for a tour in Vietnam.

Then I was sent to the `0rh Special Forces group at Fort Evans, Massachusetts.

It would be in 1970 that I would receive a call from the Pentagon. I would be asked to be an enlisted Aid. So, in 1970, I was sent back to Fort Campbell.

I re-enlisted again and this time I was sent to Saudi Arabia at Dharan. I was sent to Riyadh to run the kitchen for the training mission there.

**Me in Saudi Arabia 1971-72**

This was one of my best assignments because of the people I had to run the kitchen with me. I can still see my head waiter Chief, with his white teeth and smiling face, my two first cooks Abduhul and Abraham.

The Colonel that was the Colonel of our compound said, "You run the kitchen the way you want. If I get complaints, then, I will see what the problem is. Other than that, It's your Baby". This is where I met my old friend and colleague Colonel Charles Webb.

Every night after closing the kitchen, we would get together and play cards. We liked to play Penochie. Charles and I played as partners. I can still hear him say, "Give me your melt." I could not remember cards! Or Runs. He would not let me forget it when I did!

I really enjoyed driving from Riyad to Dharan and sliding down the sand dunes in my chevy truck that was as red as a fire wagon.

C-41 was the plane that the General would fly down to other units. He would bring us iced tea, beer wrapped in brown paper – two bottles if you wanted it!

We were offered to go on one $&$ while in the country. I went to Pakistan with Charles. Our passports were sent in advance to get processed.

Once we laned in Pakistan, I was sent to the back room. I found out that my papers were not done. I was told that I would have to get right back on the next plane and would not be able to come into the country. I was NOT happy.

I asked Charles, "You're a Colonel! See what you can do! This is NOT my fault!" The Officer said, "Why did you come here?" I replied, "To spend money!" I showed him the 'wad' that I had. He stamped it and I spent over $1500 dollars on an inlaid ivory table and a room divider!

After Saudi Arabia, I was sent to the 10th Special Forces at Ft. Devens.

Since I was just a Food Service Manager, we were not allowed to go to the Special Forces training. Not too long after that, I was sent to cook as an aid to the General at Fort Myers, MG Lang. I had a 1970 Chevy Nova 3 speed and red!

This would be the first time that I would move into a high-rise apartment on the tenth floor. I worked a few buildings from the Main Chapel at Fort Myers.

First, I was sent to Fort Dix, New Jersey. I can still see the bridge with 4,000 soldiers lined up to leave. Ten days later, we arrived in Bremerhaven, Germany - on Christmas Eve no less!

I was as 'sick as a dog' for the entire ten days. Crackers were the only thing that I could eat. On Christmas Day, I went to the movies for .25 cents and watched 'El Cid' four times. That day, I learned I would be sent to Kassel which was about 400 miles away.

I was used to having my 'jump boots'. I was wearing little 'low quarters'. I told myself, "I'm going back to 'jumping' as soon as I can for sure!"

I arrived at the outfit and reported to the mess Hall. What a dump! Those who ran the place were no better!

I took another short burst and transferred to the 509th Infantry in Aintz to a larger Mess Hall that had over a thousand men. I was the night baker and had two others that would assist with slicing slabs of bacon that would be cooked for breakfast. We worked our 'ass off'.

One night the Dining Room had a little 45 record players. I used to take my 'cake spatula' and 'stick it' so that when the music stopped, it would not shut off, but would play it over and over again. Simon and Garfunkel had one of my favorite songs, "Sounds of Silence".

**The Sound of Silence**
Hello, darkness, my old friend
I've come to talk with you again
Because a vision softly creeping
Left its seeds while I as sleeping
And the vision that was planted in my brain
Still remains
Within the sound of silence.

In restless dreams I walked alone
Narrow streets of cobblestone
Neath the halo of a streetlamp
I turned my collar to the cold and damp
When my eyes were stabbed by the flash of a neon light
That split the night
And touched the sound of silence.

And in the naked light I saw
Ten thousand people, maybe more
People talking without speaking
People hearing without listening
People writing songs that voices never share
No on dared
Disturb the sound of silence.

"Fools," said I, "You do not know
Silence like a cancer grows
Hear my words that I might teach you
Take my arms that I might reach you."
But my words like silent raindrops fell
And echoed in the wells of silence.

And the people bowed and prayed
To the neon god they made
And the sign flashes out its warning
In the words that it was forming
And the sign said, "The words of the prophets
Are written on the subway walls
And the tenement halls
And whispered in the sounds of silence."

Thanksgiving Eve, we put twenty turkeys into one of the large vats. These were used to make 'soap' that we would melt to clean the floors. We cooked these turkeys in those vats, taking breaks, and 'shooting the shit' with each other. The kitchen was at floor level next to the outside walls. We didn't pay attention to 'nothing'!

The soap suds made bubbles and we got more turkeys and kept on working. When our Boss came to work on Thanksgiving, he was shocked that it was going to be a 'joyful' day!

The Army must have paid the farmers and they must have made a lot of money! The Army was messing up their beautiful fields there!

**Vietnam**

My Sergeant called me into his office with a few others. We were being sent to Fort Dix, New Jersey for training and would be sent to Vietnam.

When I got set up, I was told that I could not go because I was NOT a U.S. Citizen. I told them, "Make me a U.S. Citizen!"

Then I took another short-term blast and had 2 more years added to my time.

I became a U.S. Citizen in Atlanta Georgia, Then I was sent to Fort Dix to join the 'gang'.

It was a long flight to Vietnam. We were then sent in many different directions. I was sent to Camtho which was a small compound called Eaking compound.

**My Upgrade**

The Boss sent me to see the Mess Sergeant and I will never forget him! He told me that the Mess officer used to be a 'chef 'at the Club 21 in New York City. He felt that we could 'mesh together'. I said, "Hell yes, I can 'mesh' with lots of Colonels and the Generals!"

I loved the job!

Every night after the meal, one of the Colonels used to open the door and say' "Great meal Sgt. Mongeau!"

I was made a Staff E-6. My Chief Officer taught me a lot and I listened well.

**The Birthday Cake**

We made birthday cakes for the brass. One particular night, my Mess Officer let me put the finishing touches on the cake. He told me, "This colonel is a 'real dick' and I want you to put a "Dick and two pairs of balls on this cake!"

He would NOT be my Mess officer the next day. One of the Majors became my new boss.

One day, he came in and told me that Senator Ted Kennedy was coming to spend two weeks with us.

**Ted Kennedy**

Since I ran the General's dining facility in Cantho, I really enjoyed the chance to meet dignitaries, including Ted Kennedy who came for a week.

The special memories of all the special ceremonies still live in my heart to this day. The Colonels knew the "Kennedy Family" from Massachusetts.

Each night after the meals, we broke out the Brandy sniffers. I was a "Special Handler" for them. I would wrap the Brandy up each night until the next time we would use it.

My new Mess officer told me there would be a helicopter that would come to pick up Mr. Kennedy. He would be coming to look around the area.

I made a special breakfast for him. The chopper then arrived with two pilots. I said, "What a pleasant surprise! You must have answered the 'call for new pilots! Great to see you CW-3 flying BIG shots around! JPE you keep in touch from now on, okay!?!"

Mr. Kennedy finally came out. The pilot asked me if I could come along with them. I was now back with those that were in our same platoon in 1962 at Fort Campbell. I will never forget that trip. I will treasure this memory forever!

After Vietnam I was sent to Fort Deven, Massachusetts. I was assigned to the 10 Special Forces Group in a large mess hall. These cats were calling us 'dumb ass bakers'. I told the Commander, "Without us 'dumb asses' you 'cats' would not be around!"

I was then sent to the 68th Engineer Company. It was the best thing. The first Sergeant and I got along! We could both speak French! He said, "You can stay here with me for a while!"

## The 68th Engineer Company - Award

My first boss was a skinny little guy, Jose Perez. I really like him! He made me a First Cook because of my being a cook in Vermont. We used to get monthly inspections from the Big Shot at headquarters.

One night, we were all called into the kitchen. We were told, "I'm sure you know we are going to inspect things in the morning. Clean everything spotless!"

Since I was the First Cook that would be on duty in the morning, I had a lot of work to do!
In the morning, I was in our parking lot which was just across the street.

There was a big dude and the Sergeant called Web Turner that showed up. When I saw them, I ran right up the big dude and said, "SP/4 Claude Mongeau reporting!" I was shaking and nervous.

He said, "What's the matter with you? Don't you have a pair of balls!? Follow me around and write down all the stuff that I find!" He went around and stuck his hand in the dumpster and into the cans. Then he stuck his hand in the garbage can and pulled out a carrot with the tip on it and bit into it and said, "We CANNOT through food away!"

Once he wrote up the report he said, 'This is one of the cleanest grease traps I've seen in a long time. Tap me on the shoulder! I will see you next month."

We won the best of the month award.
Jose was happy.

The Commander 1st Lt. James W. Crysel was happy!

# OUR MOTTO

## Chapter 6 – Above the Rest

The Company Commander, Lt James W. Crysel was a great guy. We would do anything that he asked of us. Our goal was to be 'Above The Rest"!

I was stationed at Fort Campbell, Kentucky in August 1962 and remained there until the end of 1964.

I had gone from Private to a SP/5 First cook. I was a shift leader and I went from U.S. status to R.A..

When I re-enlisted I received about $400 as a bonus and a month after that I was sent to Germany.

## GERMANY

I approached the Red Cross to get some money until I could get to my next assignment in Kassel at the 6ith Transportation outfit. All they would give me was $10 dollars.

The Officer of the day was a Warrant officer and he said, "You look like a trusted soldier, here is $20 and you can send it to me when you get paid."

I stayed in touch with him all the way until his passing. So, I am a 'Santa Claus' myself.

If I could recoup all I have given away, I would be all set.

My stay in Kassel was not long. I wanted to get back in the Airborne, so I could get my $55 back. I made it to Mainz and into the $2^{nd}$ $509^{th}$ which was in a large consolidated dining facility as the night baker and cook.

Being a night baker meant I worked 12-hour shifts within a 1,500 person consolidated Dining Facility. I had a lot of bacon to slice back then, lots of it!

It was a good time in my life. I still to this day, dream about it.

# ADVENTURES

## Chapter 7 – Other Adventures

I remember going to Canada for my Uncle Norman's wedding in my 1964 little VW Bug with Patsey my wife who was pregnant.

I remember Germany on the Patch arriving in Bremerhaven on Christmas Eve, in 1964.

I was in Fort Carson Colorado for about three months. I bought a house on Gina Drive. I hated the place. The E07 in charge of the large Dining facility had other E07's that did not care and would stab you in the back.

**MY CARS**

I owned several different cars in my lifetime:

1953 Chevy – Ugly green (I HATE GREEN!)

1956 Ford Crown Victoria

1959 Dodge - beautiful black and Red

1960 Oldsmobile Ninety-Eight  - White

# MY TRAVELS

## Chapter 8 – New Mexico

I got a call one day from my old commander. This time from the big Pentagon Office. He asked me if I would like to go to be an enlisted man to a M.G. that was down in White Sands, New Mexico. I said, "Yes Sir!" And off I went.

Once I reported for duty, this man came up to me and said, "Are you sure that you want this job?!" I asked, "Why do you ask?" He replied, "You're the second person that has applied for this job and the first did not last!"

So here I went to the Sergeant Major White. I met the General Arthur Sweeney and Mrs. Sweeney.

I would go to work each day and make a stop at the golf course and pick up balls and hit them before I went to work. I told myself, "I love this place!"

I moved into 414 Atlas Street. This was three houses down from my old friend, Veronica. I still have good memories of this special time.

## MY CONNECTION TO PRESIDENT HARRY TRUEMAN

Mrs. Sweeney had been the Secretary to Harry Truman. I stayed with them for two years.

During my time off I met a Specialist 4th class who was a master wood maker at the craft shop. I decided to make two end tables and a coffee table for my quarters, and a seven-drawer dresser.

My buddy used to say, 'measure twice and check three times!"

When it came to put all the drawers together, somehow, I messed up! Once I glued them and put them in, they were all four inches too long!

When it came to put the fronts together, my buddy said instead of wood, I have some medal mesh that is extra that I think would look good. So, I used that mesh, and I was so proud of my end tables.

I decided to take one home and show the General and Mrs.

Sweeney. One Mrs. Sweeney saw my piece, she came and kicked it and started to cry. She left the kitchen and went to her room. After a while, she came back and said, "We have worked all our life and we wanted beautiful things."

She thought I had 'copied' her furniture. I wanted to just 'quit' right then. I waited for a while. Then one night, we had a party and this Admiral said, "Sergeant, do you have a cup of tea that you could make for me?"

I went and boiled some water and put the bag in the cup. I brought the tea to the Admiral, prancing in and he said, "Thank you!"

Mrs. Sweeney said, "You're disgusting" right out loud to everyone. I marched into the kitchen. That was the last straw. I left the household the next day and never went back.

I remember Mrs. Sweeney making the General take her to the craft shop and she gave my friend a 'lashing'.
I had always wanted to go to Alaska. Mrs. Sweeny called the Sergeant Major to make sure that I DIDN'T go to Alaska!"

I had two choices: Greece or Hawaii.

# THE DREAM COME TRUE

## Chapter 9 – Hawaii

Hawaii here I come! I was assigned to Fort Quad at the 25th Infantry Brigade in a Big dining Hall. M.G. Brooks was one of my old squad leaders and Platoon Sergeant SFC. Scott and SCF Schutte were back at Fort Campbell when I first went to Ft. Campbell.

Then one day I got a call from Fort Shafter. They knew that I was an enlisted aide. They asked if I would like to come down for an interview for the commanding General Donnelly P. Bolton.

"Yes Sir!" I got the job right away.

General and Mrs. Bolton were the nicest couple I have ever worked for. I moved to Fort Shafter and worked there for two years until promoted to Warrant officer in 1985. I was sent to Quartermaster School at Fort Lee, Virginia.

After this school, I was sent to Fort Bragg and was scheduled to go to an Artillery outfit. When I reported, this 'cat' said, "We don't want no O.G. or W.G. here!"

I went to the big shot CWO-4 in charge. He sent me to DISCOM and it turned out to be a great unit. Great people and I became the $82^{nd}$ Airborne Division Food Command Food Advisor.

**THE BEST DINING FACILITY AWARD**

It was at Fort Bragg, that I was fortunate to have a good crew of soldiers that excelled. I have fond memories of this to this day. FORSCOM Best Dining Facility, and we were the 'runner UP' in the best dining facility in the ARMY in 1977. I was also the first to take a culinary team to the Fort Lee Culinary Art Culinary Competition with B. G. Leroy Sudduth.

During this time, I went to work one morning and my Sergeant Major said to me, "The Commanding General from the Big shed made a rule that if someone were to triple jump, they would be sent to the leg unit in FORSCOM. At that time, the CG and a 6-boss were in line for soldiers who wanted to call complaints or whatever they wanted to vent about.

This meant that I was going to lose over a hundred of my best dining facility managers.

I went home. Then I called the 6-Boss General Werner, myself. This was a 4 stars office. I said, "I cannot lose my best managers just because they were hurt and could not jump. If you only would replace them one on one, I could see it!"

All the while we were still competing for the grand prize of the Phillip A. Connelly Competition, the Best in the Army. Then I got orders to be stationed in of all places, Alaska!

# WAY UP NORTH!

## Chapter 10 – Alaska

In March 1979, I packed up and made tracks for Alaska.

I told my team if they won the Connelly that year, I would meet them in Los Vegas.

During my trip to Alaska, I called the inspection team on the Alaska Highway and wished them well.

I arrived on Mother's Day in 1975, to Fort Richardson to replace a Warrant that had been there for five years.

I was promoted to a WO-2 before leaving Fort Bragg.

I was supposed to be in transition for a couple of months before the old guard left. After two weeks, I said, "I'm going fishing! Do whatever you want. This is my baby now and if I mess up, I will take the 'rift-raft!" I did NOT care!

During this time, I had requested my old Sergeant Major to come with me also to Alaska. We started a program in Alaska that had never been done before. We established a culinary arts team to go compete in Fort Lee Virginia.

I had to go work in an old dining hall forty miles away. We didn't fare well in that competition the first time we competed, but it was a 'learning curve". Just like any competition, it takes time to practice, practice, and 'it takes funds'. We won eleven years in a row.

**Me with first place award– in Vancouver, British Columbia**

My then wife said, "You care more about the Army than us!" So, I lost my marriage to the military in 1980. I sent my wife and two kids back to Clarksonville, Tennessee, and I kept on charging.

# MY NEW CHAPTER

## Chapter 11 – Beginning Again

I had to sleep in my Old 1975 Country Squire station wagon for just a little while. After I found a place, instead of just feeling sorry for myself, or drinking like all the others that were getting divorced, I decided to do something!

**MY MACRAME**

I started to make Macrame. These were hangings made from ropes for plants and other things.

I made the largest 1500 to 2000 feet Macrame using cord that had burnt glass that was drilled into it in three stages high. I sold these for $500 each and I could not make them fast enough.

In my quarters I got a ladder and set up a hook. I would start from the top and work my way down. Sometimes there would be 72 strands that needed to wrap around into a knot. It was very complicated, but I love it to this day!

It was so dry that I had a slow cooker and I put water into it. I set it on the carpet. One night I woke up to the smell of my cooker. It had burned a hole all the way to the floor and it was smelling. I paid for the repairs. Then, no more slow cookers for me!

**MAIZIE**

One day I went to the draft shop. The gal in charge said, "I got someone you should meet. She worked in the dining facility. One Saturday, Maizie was introduced to me with her two daughters Renee and Denise. Her son, Toby, was working as a pizza man and he is still making great pizzas to this day! Maizie and I started dating right away.

In 1981 I retired with twenty years of service in the Army.

# BECOMING A BAKER

## Chapter 12 – My New Life

In April 1982 I was officially retired. I had been a baker in the Army and I wanted to learn more about 'French Pastries. I went into this new bakery called Parlez Vous Francias Bakery in Anchorage, Alaska.

My old friend Carl Eid was a master pastry chef that used to teach at the UAA. I became close friends with him, and he had recommended that I go there.

The lady came to the country and said, "May I help you?" I said, "My old friend recommended that I come and see you. Do you need any help? " She went inside. I heard her husband say, "I don't need any help!" I spoke a few words in French, since, after all, I was a 'frog"! I went to work the next day and for the next two years.

## MY PLACE IN NEWFOUNDLAND

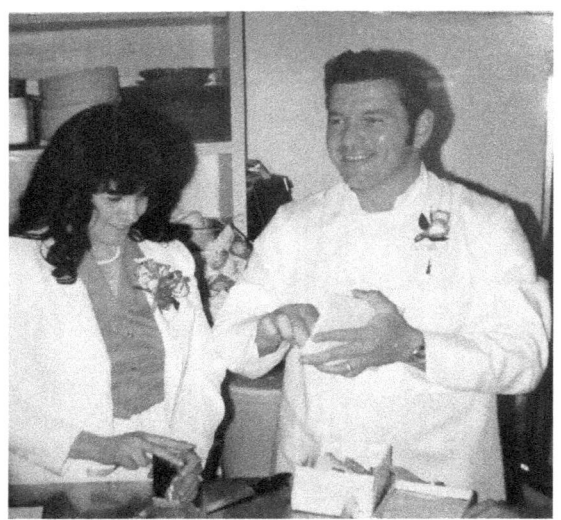

Me and Mazsie

I was called a Moudi Canadian. In June 1983 Maisie and I tied the knot for the second time and got married again to Maizie. I got on a plane and went to visit her folks with her. The lived in New Foundland. She had not seen them in over twenty-five years!

I bought a piece of land there where my wife was born. I hope someday to go back to see what it looks like.

# STORM CLOUDS

## Chapter 13 – My Biggest Trial

Maize was a wonderful wife, and mother. During our 27 years together, we made it through many trials and tribulations. Like everyone married, we had good times and we had bad times.

As we aged, it was obvious Maize was dealing with some health issues. This made life more difficult for her. On September 5, 2010, she said to me, "I'm dying. I don't want to have pain, and no more surgeries!" She asked, "How come the kids don't like us anymore?" I will never forget this, as long as I live.

The final straw happened when I went to work on September 10, 2010. I had a sense that something was wrong, but I had to go to work.

When I walked into my boss's office, I told my boss, "My wife is not well! I am concerned about her, but I am here!" I wanted to go home but I stayed at work until the end of my shift.

That evening when I did get home, I found her hanging off the gallery. At the entrance of my driveway, I could see her hanging by a rope. When I entered, I found a note on the two-by four that said, "I love you more than anything. Take care of my bunny and fuzzy!"

She had made her decision and had taken her action.

According to my neighbor, this happened just about a half hour before I got home.

To this day, I am in 'la la land' wishing I could do this over. I blame myself, and there is nothing that I can do to bring her back!

If there are angels, I know they now have a good angel up there with them. I hope someday we will meet again at the Golden Gate.

When I went to my boss, he told me to get the hell out of his office.
I really think my wife had cancer. I requested an autopsy, but none was done.

After three months I went to the medical office and asked why they did not do an autopsy. They said it wasn't necessary. So, we will never know if she had cancer or not.

Now I am on the B.C. ferry and wondering 'Why"? Why did all of this happen. The only one that knows is the headmaster upstairs.

I drove from Paret Hardy to Victoria B. C. There were beautiful and expensive 'shacks' These homes were nothing I would ever be able to afford. I waited for a ride. I knew if I didn't get one, I would try again. I was out of choices.

One of my assignments was when I was hired by a contractor to run the kitchen in Shemya, Alaska. This was approximately 1,700 miles away located by Reeves Airline. I caught the last flight before being forced to ride a C-130 for six hours. I was told you are going to love it there. There is a 'girl' behind every tree. I got off the plane. I saw a big runway, there were four bushes by a little pond of water. I went into the kitchen and was greeted by my old boss. To my surprise there were five ladies working there.

**MY MEDIVAC**

I would leave there in twenty months on a medivac. I had a heart attack. I was given 15 nitro pills and that got me to Providence Hospital. There was 90% of my right vein blocked and 70% blockage on the left. Three weeks later, I would go back there.

## MY DAY AS A MINISTER

I was made a minister for one day. That day I married two of my friends that had been there for years.

I know friends that spent thirty years on that island.

I loved my job there.

One of my old friends ran all the generators there until he was 90 years old.

# GOING HOME!

## Chapter 14 - Full Circle

My decision to move back to Vermont would allow me to find and finally get to know Brenda. Truly the 'best' part of my life was saved for the last part of my life! Amazingly, it feels like there has never been any 'gap' in our friendship. As though, we were lifetime friends, separated only by the 'distance' of our different locations for all those years. A connection of 'hearts' our entire lives. My life came into a 'full circle' which united us back together as we were at the very start!

## Chapter 15 – LIFE LESSONS

When I think back, there are many things that bring tears to my eyes:

- Life is truly very unpredictable.

- It is the 'people' you meet that make your life 'rich'.

- It is 'looking back' that helps events to make sense.

- Faith in God and in Jesus Christ's Resurrection brings peace.

- We must 'let go' of the bad times to 'move on' in life.

- We need to be a 'friend' – this is the secret to true happiness.

The BIG TEN reduces to just two: "Love God" and Love One Another". The center of the 'wheel of life" must be loving God for this is the true purpose of our life! In the end, the only thing that will matter will be those two. The magic carpet ride of life will reunite us to the Lord in the end, and THEN we will all agree that we were created by God who loves each of us as though there were only one of us!

www.ingramcontent.com/pod-product-compliance
Lightning Source LLC
Chambersburg PA
CBHW060218050426
42446CB00013B/3105